# Nowt so daft...

## by Kieran Meehan

C000030714

Published by Meehan Cartoons

# ... as folk

www.nowtsodaft.com

Second edition.
© 2014 The author retains sole copyright
to the contents of this book. All rights reserved.

ISBN 978-0-9573082-5-1

Published by Meehan Cartoons

3

7

THINGMY ON THE PORT BOW!! You know, what's it called? Long and pointy...very fast... TORPEDO ON THE PORT BOW!!
meehan

16

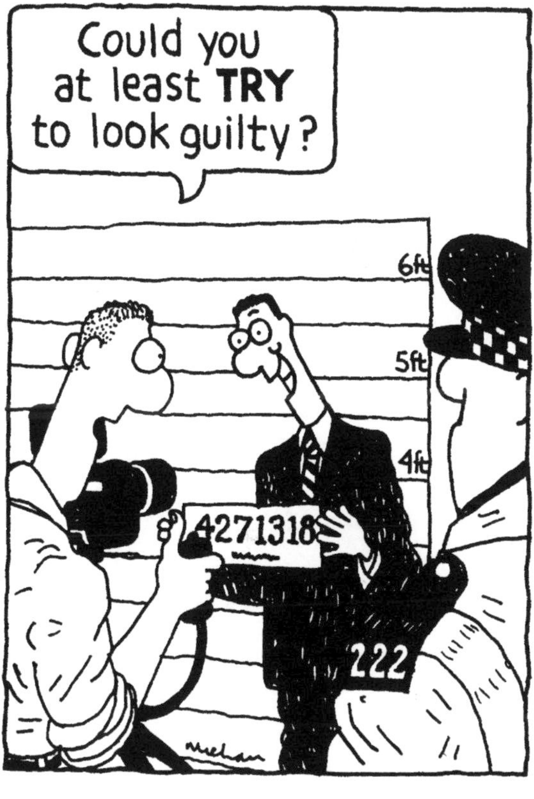
Could you at least TRY to look guilty?
6ft
5ft
4ft
4271318
222

32

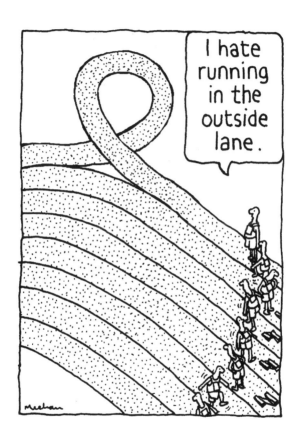

72

80

81

I was talking to that George Clooney yesterday. He is **SUCH** a name-dropper.

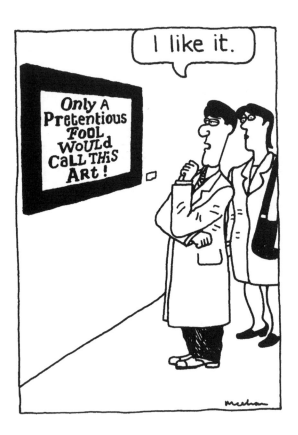

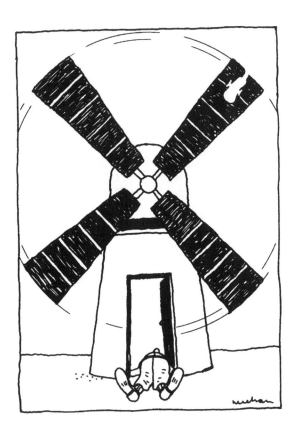

You're telling me you learned how to make fire BEFORE organising contents insurance ?!

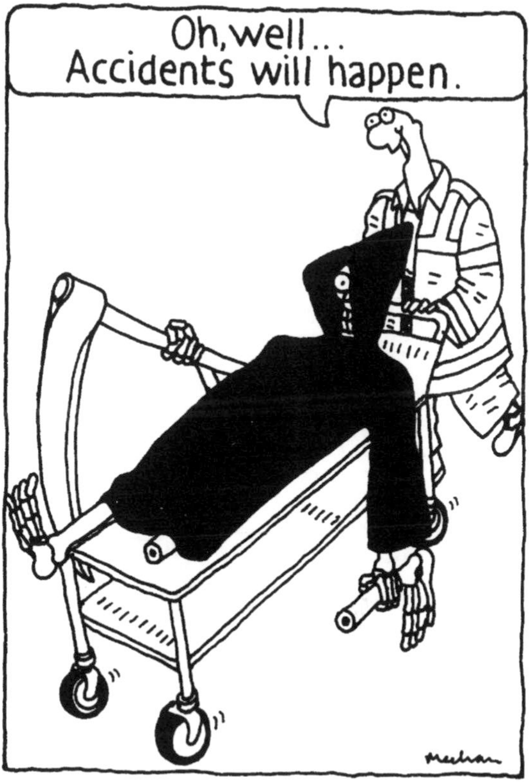
Oh, well...
Accidents will happen.

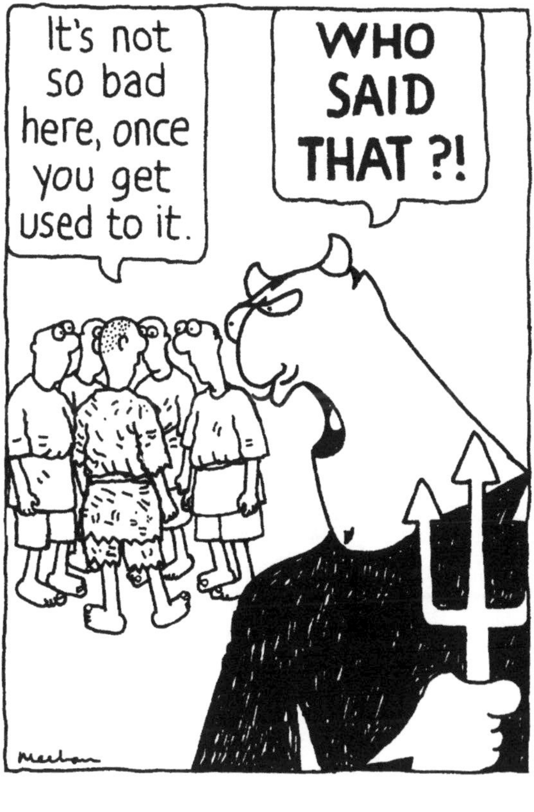
It's not so bad here, once you get used to it.
WHO SAID THAT ?!

113

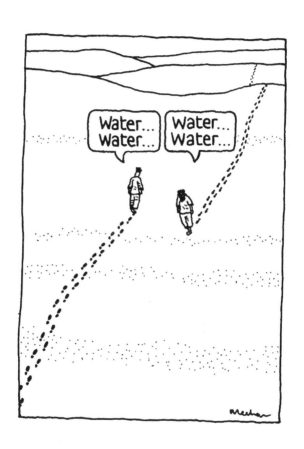

I can tell you now, you're already infringing several health and safety rules.

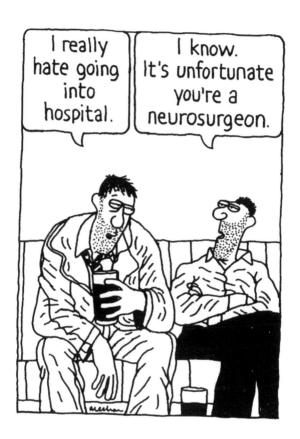

Fire, rudimentary tools, the ability for abstract thought. Bloody kids don't know they're living.
Meehan

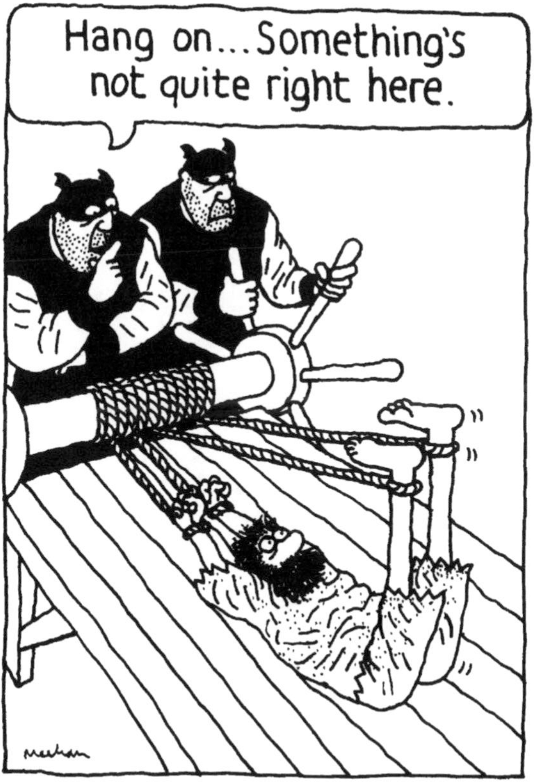
Hang on... Something's not quite right here.
meehan

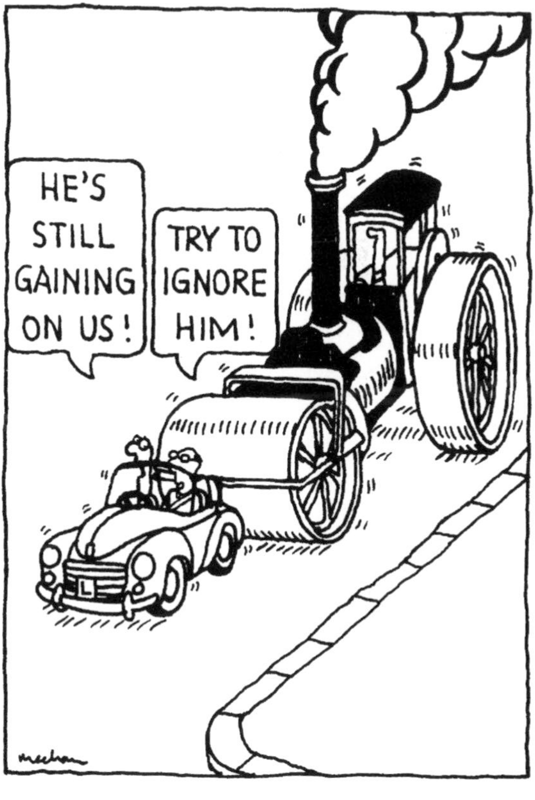
HE'S STILL GAINING ON US!
TRY TO IGNORE HIM!
L
meehan

If art is supposed to be life-affirming, why am I losing the will to live?

171

179

**www.nowtsodaft.com**

'Nowt so daft…' clothing, mugs, prints and other
merchandise can be purchased online at www.cafepress.com
Single panel cartoons can be purchased for reprints
and merchandise through Cartoon Stock at
www.cartoonstock.com

The Comic strip, 'Pros & Cons,' can be viewed and
purchased through King Features Syndicate at
www.Dailyink.com
and the Cartoonist Group at www.cartoonistgroup.com

Second edition.
© 2014  The author retains sole copyright
to the contents of this book. All rights reserved.

ISBN 978-0-9573082-5-1

Published by Meehan Cartoons

Made in the USA
Charleston, SC
17 March 2014